I Witnessed
Miracles of God

Wendell Fountain

authorHOUSE·

AuthorHouse™
1663 Liberty Drive
Bloomington, IN 47403
www.authorhouse.com
Phone: 833-262-8899

Published by AuthorHouse 12/28/2023

ISBN: 979-8-8230-2016-9 (sc)
ISBN: 979-8-8230-2015-2 (e)

Library of Congress Control Number: 2023924630

Print information available on the last page.

Any people depicted in stock imagery provided by Getty Images are models,
and such images are being used for illustrative purposes only.
Certain stock imagery © Getty Images.

This book is printed on acid-free paper.

Contents

Contents

As Gracie, the love of my life, used
to say, "There are no accidents, it's
just God acting anonymously."

Over the years, I've written on numerous topics of interest to me; however, I've never attempted to write, nor did I ever want to write about, the death of my wife--Gracie. Even writing these words is traumatic and emotionally disturbing, but God's actions and presence must not be ignored.

Though novella's, in a formal sense, are usually considered to be fictional accounts, I assure you this is not the case in this short story. It is a true account of what I saw and experienced.

What I want to share with you, is a *factual account* of an actual event that occurred on the night of April 14, 2023. The intent of this message is to bring hope and joy to all because I know beyond the shadow of a doubt that God exists and communicates with His followers. Most of us are quite familiar with prayers to God the Father in the name of Jesus, but what went on that mysterious night, defies this commonly accepted approach.

What I personally experienced and saw was not an illusion, mental aberration, nor the unfounded ramblings of a stroke victim --of which I am one. In a way, I actually died along with my wife, Gracie, on that fateful night of April 14, 2023, Later, I will more fully explain. Physically, I am still here on Earth because of my wife, Gracie, and with the help of God Almighty. God knew her limitations and mine and spared her the pain of loneliness, despair, and the deep sadness I face each day. Though it pains me greatly, but if this is for her, I am happy to make this contribution and sacrifice for the love of my life. I am thankful to God that He gave me precious hours, days and nights, even years with her in a love relationship most people only dream about. Gracie was truly unique.

With jocularity, I frequently referred to her as "The Mother of the World." She prayed for everyone on a regular basis. All during the night, she faithfully and lovingly caressed her blessed Rosary beads with Hail Mary's and Our Father's.

Now alone, I greet each day with the sadness of an of an lonely heart, but the beauty of her essence shines before me as a bright light, that leads me back to us where I believe she waits for me. Her human form no longer exits. I know of which I speak because I literally watched her dissipate before my eyes, she now resides in the bosom of God the Father.

My initial reaction to the passing of Gracie was irrational and not like me at all. I wanted to run from everything, including our lifetime of shared memories both good and bad. I was emotionally very vulnerable. I even placed our house up for sale but soon learned that was a mistake and later took it off the market.

Admittedly, our past three years together had been marred by serious physical ailment that included multitude and range of illnesses; however, it didn't take me long to convince myself I could not live in our home alone because we built it together, and without her, I felt and feel empty and lost. Though well intended, bromides such as "the passage of time will make things better," "just take it one day at a time, and of course, probably the most infamous of all, "time heals all wounds" are empty platitudes that are just that—empty. None of them are even remotely reflective of the eight beatitudes of Jesus. Life is not a platitude. It is reality and reality can hit you like a Mack truck, as it did me.

There are poignant moments in time that the seen cannot be unseen. On April 14, 2023 was such a night. Gracie and I were staring into each other's eyes, as we had the first time, we met more than two decades earlier. At that moment, I knew she was slipping away and I panicked. Gracie had always insisted that her wishes that no one do anything to bring her back from eminent death be followed. In other words, she did not believe in resuscitation. I, on the other hand, did not agree with her thinking on this matter; however, I did not see harm in doing nonheroic measures to facilitate the continuance of sustaining life. When I attempted to intervene in her passing, I will never forget the disappointed and horrified look on her face. I am convinced She was prepared to meet God the Father and what I was doing, looking back now, I pray to God, she forgave me for my actions. Somehow, I even called 911 for help. As a man and human being, I could not stand by and do nothing. She often said to me, "I love you more than life itself." Gracie meant it and proved it later hat night. She called out to me to help her relocate from the her, to the office area. Without hesitation or the questioning of her motives, I complied.

At that time, I had no reason to do anything but what she asked of me. Only later did I discover her motives to move to the office area. Without my knowledge, and from what I've been told, she had asked key neighbors to look after me if she was no longer there. I've had difficulty with this from the beginning. I am convinced that if she had asked something like that of me, I would have been cautious about complying, that is, I would have expected a more definitive explanation. Regardless, I am convinced she knew her departure was eminent and she had to make sure I would be rescued by a caring and loving neighbor, by allowing entrance though a shuttered and closed window. Without me knowing, she repositioned a shutter to make sure I would be safely rescued. To the end, she did all she could to ensure my safety. Despite that, because of my ensuing stroke(s), I lay on the floor for many hours before my rescue occurred. Thank God I now have a Medical Guardian alert system in case something like this occurs again, and now that I live alone, this kind of incident can be ameliorated.

I must digress for clarity and continuity. By the time we had come to this point, Gracie, since she was a fantastic researcher and held an earned doctorate in hospital management, was acutely aware of what was to be her immediate future. Not only was she well-educated, but when younger, she had been a Registered Nurse, Nurse Practitioner, and the first P.A. (Physician's Assistant} in Binghamton, New York.

She knew what to expect was more hospitalizations, and pain would be her future going forward. She was too full of life to accept such a fate, and she knew God was the answer. Besides, she did not want me to have to sit by and observe her misery and sadness, but that never stopped her from never leaving my side when I was hospitalized, once for 23 consecutive days, after a cancer of the colon operation, even then, she only left me when hospital regulations forced her to go home. She was the most knowledgeable and effective advocate any patient could ever have, and I always eagerly awaited her daily arrival no matter how rotten I felt, her smile always contained rays of warm sunshine.

I did the same for her during her many hospitalizations. We used to joke, "It's just you and me kid." In a way, it is sad that few people ever knew how funny and humorous she could be. Gracie had a very subtle sense of humor. She loved my southern aphorisms, and sometimes she would nearly bend me over, trying to emulate something funny I had said, such as, "She looks like she's been rode hard and put to bed wet," or "I'm as full as a blue tick on a hound dog's ear." When she tried to repeat what I had just stated, it became hilarious. She had a sweetness, kindness, and tender way about her.

Regarding her humor, our wedding truly demonstrated beyond any doubt that she could be funny and persuasive in many different situations. Of course, most married couples are excited about the new road they will travel, but Gracie had friends and family from all over the country in attendance. Some of them, she had not seen in years.

Gracie was not always serious. She could laugh at herself. For example, these words are prominently displayed on the wall in our kitchen.

A
WILD
WACKY
WONDERFUL
WOMAN LIVES HERE!

Our wedding day was glorious to me. I think very few men would speak in such glowing terms, but that is how I think and feel about her. In fact, the preceding comment falls far short as a descriptor of who she was as a human being.

Obviously, needless to say, I was very proud of her. It was not that she was a woman but the woman that she was.

Gracie always worried about others. It seemed there were times she couldn't get enough information about the health, condition, or well-being those in need.

When I think of Gracie today, I always see her smiling because she was eternally happy, and upbeat. That, is some of a thousand or more things I miss most about her absence. She, with frequency, would encourage me to smile more often, because it made her happy, and when I smiled, it lessened my burden. I complied as often as possible.

She was a happy soul of good cheer and ebullience. Even before we were married, she was well-liked and helpful to others and contributed greatly to her community. One of the things she was most admired for was her incredible voice. She had a powerful delivery with impressive clarity. If she sang early in a karaoke setting, others were reluctant to follow. They often felt intimidated She sang in Las Vegas and Jamaica once and potential singers were very hesitant to follow her.

Nothing describes her better than the day of our wedding. Our ceremony lasted for more than an hour and a half, and Father Bob seemed to be in his element. When he asked her, "Do you take this man to be your lawful wedded husband?" Her reply was priceless, "I REALLY, REALLY DO!" After that, when appropriate, the congregation of more than 150 began joining in each time with that rejoinder. Everyone seemed to be enjoying themselves as frequent laughter rippled across the room.

Gracie referred to our wedding as Our "Big Fat Italian Fairytale Wedding." She borrowed the idea from the popular movie of 2002 My Big Fat Greek Wedding. Gracie and her mother prepared enough Italian food for more than 150 well-fed people.

The photo below shows Gracie in all her splendor verbally exhorting members of the congregation at the Wedding Reception to fully participate in the festivities such as the preplanned singalong. She was incredibly talented and innovative. Following was a magic act performed by our doctor friend, and later the evening was topped off with a dance contest that lasted for two hours and won by a couple of which the male was in his early 20s and his partner was in her late 80s.

The happy couple – Gracie and Wendell make their grand entrance at the Reception Hall. They were thrilled with each other and their future together.

Gracie overflowed with love during their

first dance as husband and wife.

No wedding would be complete without a wedding cake, and and our wedding one was no different. Gracie knew what she wanted and was happy with it. Her histrionics were truly icing on the cake. This was a joyous moment for Gracie. She enjoyed stuffing cake into my mouth while giggling about it.

She sang along with the wedding party songs such as Bye, Bye, Birdie, That's Amore (That's Love) made famous by the late great Dean Martin), Side By Side, and a host of others.

From left to right – Anita Mandicottott, Monica

Gracie swept across the floor while urging everyone

to sing. This was her day and she thoroughly

enjoyed every minute of that joyous night.

I must have told Gracie a dozen times or more that I
was a writer—not a singer, but if she asked something
of you, not doing what she asked, was out of the
question. That was the power of her carisma.

Gracie and Wendell transcended practically everything

as they admired the accoutrements of their union.

She had the most extraordinary beautiful hands.

Recently, I have been able to assemble more critical information about the occurrences of April 14, 2023. Since I couldn't tell whether or not Gracie was wearing her wedding ring at the time of her collapse, I searched for it, and found it in her special jewelry case in the bedroom. Hopefully, I am not reading too much into this, but to me, that is more substantive support that she was preparing for her departure. She knew that God would soon take over. At this point, I must reiterate that, before we met, Gracie had seriously considered becoming a nun. Now she can serve the Lord more fully.

Since I have digressed, it is important that you are aware of what actually transpired over those painful minutes of April 14, 2023. As I alluded earlier, I thought she and I were dying simultaneously, as a result of her heart failure and the stroke(s) that had begun to grip my body like a vise, I hoped we would go together, but obviously, God still had work for me to do. Though she was physically in the adjoining room, and how she got there, I do not know. Regardless, we maintained continuous eye contact for nearly the entire time until somehow, she made her way to me in the office. As she was dying, she tried to get to me Let me hasten to add, we never let a day go by without at least verbal recognition of our love for each other. Sometimes, it would be late in the day and either she or I or would remind the other of our oversight.

What I visually observed was truly astonishing. God took control and began answering her prayer. I actually watched as her body began to dissipate from sight. When her head and neck were no longer visible, I knew she would not be back. In fact, it was as if God had switched on His heavenly vacuum to remove her human remains and Gracie quickly vanished from my eyesight. I saw a silhouette from behind the "vacuum" and when finished, she and the apparition streaked upward into the heavens. Gracie was headed home to her eternal reward.

It was about then, harsh reality engulfed my heart, mind, and soul. Now, I must thank God again and again for allowing me the privilege of sharing her life with me over many years (a total of twenty-two) from the time she passed on April 14, 2023. She was incredibly very special to me. When it came to financial matters, I pawned all of that off upon her. I used to joke with her about being the "Minister of Finance" which meant she had all the responsibility for all things relative to financial issues and just about everything else relating to running the household. I used to tell her that her job was like becoming a member of the Supreme Court—a lifetime appointment. If I only knew then what I know now, that is one crack I would never have used.

She was a wonderful cook thanks to her mother and grandmother both of whom were great at preparing meals; although, Gracie learned from them both--mostly as an observer. Italians seem to gravitate into that direction. She took great delight in creatively concocting new things for us to enjoy. I always complimented her for being so creative.

Gracie and I used to make light of the number of years we had been together compared to many family members and friends, and she would usually retort something like, "It's not the number of years we've been together, it is what we have experienced during our time as a couple. Considering what we've done in such a short time, what we have accomplished, and the places we've lived, we have probably lived two lifetimes," she would lightly scoff with a smile and a light-hearted chuckle. Even then, in my heart and mind, I had a dread of one of us living without the other. Since we had met late in life, it was a given that one of us would be left without the other. Such thoughts I repressed because I never even considered a life without Gracie. She was the picture of health until about three years ago when the cardiologist used the term "heart failure". That term was unexpected and very unsettling. Up until then, we had been going to see him for many years, and that condition had never been discussed. Now, he tells me that I, too, have heart failure like Gracie with an ejection fraction of 25%, which is very low. Speaking of cardiologists, on a recent appointment I was told about the broken heart syndrome. If you think that my pain, remorse, and sadness can be disregarded because a name has been applied to this horrible condition, you are sadly mistaken. Gracie was my reason to be, my life, hopes, and dreams that were intertwined within her and into my very being.

I have little doubt that there are skeptics and doubters about my proclamations, and you have every reason to think and feel that way, but I assure you, I am of sound mind and none of the medical professionals with whom I am in contact on a regular basis question my mental acuity. In fact, the series of strokes I encountered had very limited negative effect on my physiology. About the only thing that has changed is the color and texture of my hair. My grey-brown hair is now all white and rather unruly. Other than that, most people with whom I come in contact are amazed I suffered strokes. Yes, I move more slowly now and my balance needs improvement. I will more fully address this in greater detail in the postscript that follows.

Postscript

With the exception of Gracie not being with me any longer, physically, I'm doing okay despite having more strokes while driving later on the evening of April 21st that resulted in damage to our vehicle. Why I was behind the wheel of an automobile, at that point, I did not know. Gracie had passed away on the 14th. Only later, I learned from my brother-in-law I was returning from having the car washed and cleaned because of the expected arrival of family members. Thankfully, no one was hurt or injured. Since now Gracie is with the Lord, it gives me immense comfort, and I know that for certain because I saw her heavenly ascension as discussed earlier. I'm just thankful God brought us together in the first place.

Nothing will ever change regarding my love and devotion to Gracie. Though, physically, we were two people, we always thought of ourselves as one. Even though marriage vows state "Until death do you part," As a human, I feel as though half of me is missing. Regardless, I will remain devoted to God and Gracie for the rest of my life, after all, she is and will always be the love of my life. Dear Lord . . . I miss her so.

This is a photo of our last anniversary together. A close look reveals she was not well even then. Behind her forced smile was pain and misery. Also, notice we were wearing our formal wedding clothes from two decades earlier. I always wore my tuxedo and she her wedding dress as we did the day of our wedding June 4,1999. She liked to think we started a new trend, and she thought it was a shame to wear her beautiful dress only once. At the time, I had no inkling that would be our last anniversary together.

Gracie always prided herself in being able to wear and fit into her wedding gown. In the photo below, because of her illness, she was less than 110 pounds—four pounds less than her target weight when we married. Her cardiologist insisted that she not exceed 112 pounds for concern about fluid retention. She looked as though she was an escapee from a German prisoner of war camp of the 1940s. I have personally known men and women who suffered from heart failure, and some of them, were quite heavy. I disagreed with the cardiologist on this, because Gracie had no room for error. For a woman who stood 5 ft'7 inches tall, she needed more muscle.

This is where I must enter uncharted territory because other than prayer, I was
not privy to how God communicated with her; therefore, that which follows is
speculative but I believe it to be rational and reasonable. For Gracie to do and
say the things she did and said on that tumultuous night, one can only presume
that God was directing her thoughts, movements, and spirit. He responded by
answering her prayer to be free of the disease that was squeezing the life out of
her body.

He responded to her physical frailties in a positive manner, and as her reward, He decided to answer the prayer of his good and faithful servant and whisked her away to her heavenly home. Gracie had always loved God deeply. There was a time when she had even seriously considered becoming a nun. As her husband, I was always very pleased she had chosen to be my wife and helpmeet instead, but it is clear that her prayers led from our earthly home to her heavenly home for eternity. I only hope and pray that she waits for me. Since time is not a consideration in the world beyond, I expect to see her upon my arrival.

Not that I expect it, even though God allowed her physical form to change and disappear, if it is according to His will, He can bring her back to me as she was, without the ravages of disease. Two people, like us, who unconditionally love each other and God so deeply must be pleasing to the Lord. Gracie and I truly believe that to be the case. She is now in her heavenly home where soon, I believe, I will be, but until then, I will continue to "sing" her praises and keep her beautiful memory alive. I love you, Gracie. It was a privilege and honor for me to be to be your husband.

Books also by Wendell Vanderbilt Fountain

The Dark side of Carmel [Fiction]

TRUMP: Man Phenomenon President [Nonfiction]

Clay Country Boy [Nonfiction Novella]

WILLOBEE'S WORLD [Fiction Novel]

Ups and Downs: That's Life on Earth! [Nonfiction Dramatic Comedy]

The New Emerging Credit Union World: Theory, Process, Practice—Cases and Application [nonfiction]

THOUGHT PROVOKING LESSONS OF LIFE: True Short Stories from the Real World [Nonfiction]

Rainbows from the Heart [Poetry]

How to Build a Southwestern House [nonfiction]

ACADEMIC SHARECROPPERS: Exploitation of Adjunct

Faculty and the Higher Education System [Nonfiction]

GRACE [Fiction Novel and Motion Picture—Grazia the Movie]

LOVE—40 [Fiction Novel]

THE CREDIT UNION DIRECTOR: Roles,

Duties, and Responsibilities--nonfiction

www.wendellfountain.com [Website]

Printed in the United States
by Baker & Taylor Publisher Services

Printed in the United States
by Baker & Taylor Publisher Services